Moving African Landscapes

VOL 1

Dr. Tokie Laotan-Brown

© 2023 by Arbi Press, a division of Siyanda Africana Institute
44 Evans Avenue, Binghamton NY 13903, USA
119 Ndidem Isang Iso, Calabar, Cross River State, Nigeria

ISBN: 978-1-961929-00-5

Typesetting: Miroslav Suster

CONTENTS

ACKNOWLEDGEMENT

University of Nova Goricia, UNISCAPE, Arbi Press, DG Green Foundation, Vernacular Heritage Initiative, Beaded Ladies and Black Daughter.

Moving African Landscape Competition Entrants and Chapter Contributors.

MANAGING CHANGE, KNOWING HISTORY

Marco Acri
University of Nova Gorica

The need to tackle landscape as a moving asset has become increasingly relevant by acknowledging its potential loss, thus in parallel with a growing conservation concern. Even though nature is itself constantly generously and ruthlessly mutating, accepting either radical or gradual replacement by a new over an old. What is known is exceptional and witnesses the existence on earth, what may come is uncertain and possibly not as good as the previous. Within this perspective we have formulated solid theories and practices on conservation, protection, regeneration, that are meant to save us and ourselves and our traces on earth more than nature. We know that nature will continue, maybe different, maybe from a new generating push, but we do not know if we will be there to witness this. Most human beings in centuries have been constructing their habitats by resisting, adapting, rejecting or pretending to dominate nature, finally achieving a set of "comfortable" knowledge that pushes for conservation. In this perspective, if for many decades from the mid 20th century the preservation efforts have been focused on the built heritage and the built environment, as a consequence to the devastating effects of World Conflicts, later a new concern for conservation has taken place, in specific for the environment, for nature, for all other living beings. The effects of human resistance and rejection have become so impactful to reach the threshold between reversibility and irreversibility (a very important dichotomy in the conservation theory) asking for scientists and practitioners to look for solutions. Today we increasingly hear about the concepts of adaptive reuse, circular economy, nature-based solutions, resilience within the big umbrella of sustainability, finally realizing that most of these terms fall back to the periods of resistance and adaptation, namely when human beings were looking for moderate synergic co-action measures. in fact adaptive reuse is a modern simplification of the millennial capacity of living beings to transform assets to their need; circular economy recalls the millennial *oikos*, management of the house, perfect balance between efficiency and efficacy in the maximization of efforts and waste; nature-based solutions retrace the empirical adaptations of nature to nature and later of humans to nature, transforming the latter with a mutual benefit; resilience reminds about the persistent instinctive behavior of communities to use and not abuse as a guarantee for the future. The impertinent and superficial voracity of human individuality, riding excessive confidence of supermanagement entrusted to the free market and its global speed, has rapidly corroded the trust on traditions and traditional knowledge, namely the same that we need to refer to any sustainability talk.

Landscapes are paradigmatic as well as brutal symptoms of such phenomenon. Landscape, either defined as panoramas or as an ensemble of assets and associations for individuals or groups, is the sentinel of change, like the rose to predict the vineyard disease. The change of landscapes and the connection of such change with the loss of traditional knowledge has moved the University of Nova Gorica and its course in Cultural Heritage Studies, jointly with UNISCAPE, University Network for the Implementation of the EU Landscape Convention, and Merging Ecologies and with the support of other partners, to organize an educational session at this year Biennale di Architettura di Venezia in its 18th Edition entitled "The Laboratory of the Future" and curated by Leslie Lokko. The Biennale is indeed inspired by the role of Africa in telling new narratives, that often are old ones simply forgotten in the globalized world. The session, entitled "African landscape on the move - Moving African Landscape", was meant to credit the African landscapes as still able to tell resilient stories, that are made of constant dialogue and cooperation with the environment, with nature and its forces and where human beings are actors that creatively innovate by doing keeping an apparently chaotic balance with natural pushes and speeds. The session followed the outcomes of the first edition of the UNISCAPE Forum, held in 2022 in Bruxelles at the NEB, New European Bauhaus, Festival, UNISCAPE will take this occasion to launch the **Uniscape Forum** for students and early-stage researchers by opening up the dialogue with their peers from Africa to exchange and discuss together the challenges of Landscape research, share their landscape stories, imaginaries, hopes and ambitions.

As stated by Lesley Lokko, Africa is "...the place on this planet where all issues of equity, race, hope and fear converge and merge. Anthropologically we are all Africans. And what happens in Africa happens to all of us..."

The initiative benefits from the experience of the University of Nova Gorica and the Cultural heritage Studies programme to investigate in landscape research the connections among adaptive reuse, traditional knowledge, nature based solutions and circular practices, both in urban and in rural contexts, feeding and taking from the conservation theory and the intimate sustainability of cultural and natural heritage.

INTRODUCTION

Knowledge is like a garden. If it is not cultivated, it cannot be harvested

— **African Proverb**

The Moving African Landscapes Volume 1 examines a broad spectrum of natural and cultural concepts, sensory responses, and innate perceptions experienced, learned, and recalled by Africans within their environment. Photographers, Architects, Lecturers, and Visual Artists are all interested in articulating their ideas of what *Moving African Landscapes* means to them. The authors capture their intuitive understanding of how they observed the interaction of their landscapes, built environment, kins, community, spacial behaviors, social practice, and political hierarchies across ancestral timelines influencing their everyday culture. As African DNA is carried across oceans into other lands through food, clothing, and communal nature, their toponymy and tacit reverie become one. This web of connecting fractal elements is experienced through these contributions in this volume, from the built environment to landscapes of all manners of expression in different voices and depictions.

TREE FOR LIFE

There are trees in my mummy's office. Some are tall and the others are short. Some of the trees have flowers that are pink, green, yellow, white and purple in colour.

Trees are wonderful because they protect us from harsh weather. Some times, I hide under the tree in my mummy's office when it is sunny. The trees protect me from having fever caused by the hot sun, my life is therefore preserved through the help of the trees. Also, trees give life to birds by providing shelter for them and their babies; a place to call home. I also use the flower that falls from the trees to decorate my mummy's office, by putting it in a flower vase to beautify her office. I also put these flowers in my hair, Tj's and my sister's hair to make us look like princesses.

Also, trees gives us fruits and foods, which make us strong and healthy just like me. Living things depend on trees for their survival. Everyone should plant a tree for life to be preserved and nurtured.

Written by Inioluwa Eniola Agboola at 5 years 11months
She is now 9 years old
Based in Lagos, Nigeria.

CHAPTER 1

ENIYAN!

Dr Tokie Laotan-Brown
Heritage Architect
Merging Ecologies Studio
Lagos, Nigeria ꕤ

The divine language spoken by the Creator, the word for "humanity" is ENIYAN. It means, "custodian of earth." The word emphasizes purpose. We are not the rulers of Earth, we are the custodians (the maintenance workers) of the planet. That is our purpose on Earth. We are eniyan."- Iya's of Awo Ogboni Funfun in Abeokuta, 2014

In African societies, knowledge is collectively and communally owned, not monopolized or standardized by individuals. While community members share knowledge, specific elders from the community remain its assigned custodians. Eniyan as part of their natural and cultural landscape are intertwined and cannot negate haptic reverie as part of analytical knowledge. This haptic recognition can be identified as inferred information as opposed to express learning.

Because we are Eniyan! As Eniyan we are one with our Landscapes.

Cultural linkages between place names and environmental knowledge, toponymy as a language can reveal oral narrations of places and topographical attributes which Eniyan use in teaching their young about their localities and their landscapes. These moving African Landscapes intertwine songs, proverbs, storytelling and rituals embodying place makers within them as the knowledge that are performative in nature and divinity.

Because we are Eniyan! As Eniyan we are one with our Landscapes.

As Eniyan, we must teach the importance of the elements of water, earth, air and fire. As Eniyan, we are governed by these energies as it affects our moving African landscapes.

CHAPTER 2

MOVING AFRICAN LANDSCAPES DESIGN NARRATIVE

ORI

ORI: Moving Within Self
Designed by: Nate Robert-Eze, MUD
Nigeria

SUMMARY

'ORI' encapsulates the exploration of self, a concept deeply rooted in our shared human experience. As a designer, I have delved into the essence of Yoruba culture, connecting with the teachings of Kọ́lá Abímbọ́lá, an esteemed Nigerian scholar, and the foundational work of Carl Jung, the pioneer of analytical psychology. The intersection of these unique perspectives fuels this concept.

WHAT IS "ORI"?

In Yoruba philosophy, 'Ori' is an intuitive guide, personal destiny, and the potential for achieving a good life. As a symbol of personal divinity, 'Ori' draws parallels with Jung's concept of Individuation, the quest for self-realization by understanding and integrating the unconscious. Although cultures vary, the longing to uncover our inner selves and destinies remain universal, tying us together in our collective human experience.

'ORI' manifests as a collection of four landscapes/hardscapes designed with the design language – Human Scale, Parametric Design, AfroFuturism, and Biomimicry. Each space is crafted to invoke thought, kindle emotion, and inspire action, ultimately leading us on a journey of self-discovery and collective evolution.

'ORI' is not just a design; it's a journey – a pathway to understanding our true selves, a quest for inner harmony. As we connect deeper within, we spark a contagion of connection, a ripple effect that connects us all in a wave of shared consciousness and mutual understanding. As we navigate these landscapes, we move not just physically, but spiritually and psychologically, stepping closer to our destinies, pushing humanity forward, together.

THE SPACES

The Botanical Garden, a haven of natural beauty, stimulates introspection. The Golf Course, a mental landscape, challenges strategic thinking and self-evaluation. The Riverwalk, a physical pathway, encourages exploration and environmental connectivity. Lastly, the Water Show, an aspirational landscape, evokes a sense of awe and limitless potential.

THE MOTIF

Each of the landscapes is subtly imbued with an African motif, reflecting the teachings of Jung and Abímbọ́lá. These motifs guide us through the four stages of self-discovery, represented in black and white logos, symbolizing our inner darkness and light.

1. Unawareness: An unfilled left circle against a filled right, symbolizing the initial state dominated by external influences, with inner understanding yet to be discovered.

2. Initial Self-Exploration: The right side split into quadrants, marking the start of true self-discovery, inspired by Jung's concepts and Abímbọ́lá's exploration of Ori.

3. Increased Self-Awareness: A filled and quartered left side symbolizing an in-depth understanding of self, independent of external influence.

4. Self-Understanding: A fully filled left circle, free of quadrants, signifying a complete embrace and understanding of one's true self. Right side not filled in to show

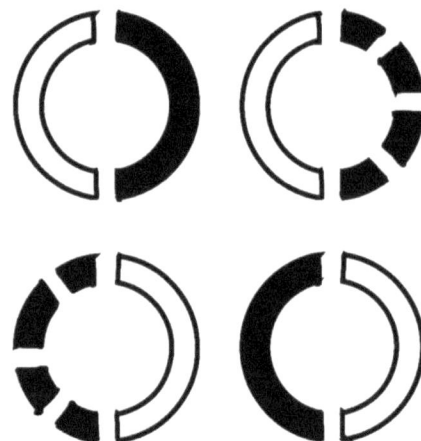

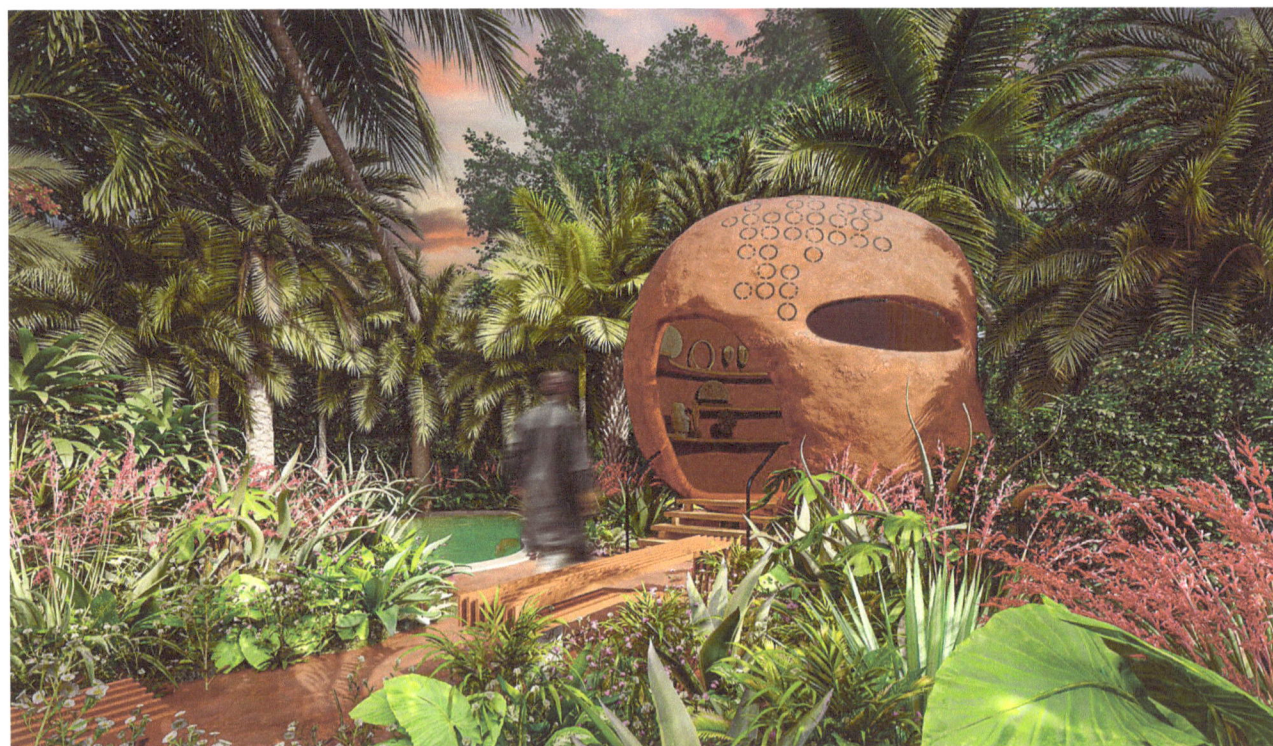

CHAPTER 3

THE OLD MEETING THE NEW IN EAST AFRICAN COUNTRIES

Justicia Caesaria Kiconco is an Architect, from Uganda living in Rwanda, with a deep passion on how to bridge architecture and everyday life, specifically in the areas of architectural history, heritage, sustainable environment and education, using design methods, visual representation, textual analysis, and strategies for action. She actively seeks to create connections and enact positive change through architecture.

Zanzibar (Tanzania), Kenya, Kampala (Uganda) and Musanze (Rwanda).

The concept of the old meeting the new in the context of Zanzibar, Kampala, and Musanze in East Africa can provide insights into the potential future of these regions. Each location represents a different stage of development, showcasing the evolution and transformation of their landscapes over time.

Landscape refers to the physical, natural, and cultural features. African landscape is deeply intertwined with human history and culture. Also termed as "mama land" refers to one's homeland, ancestral land, or the land that holds cultural and emotional significance. It represents a deep connection to one's roots, traditions, and identity. Landscape encompasses a broader sense of belonging and cultural heritage tied to the land. It represents a connection to one's heritage, a sense of belonging, and a cultural anchor that shapes individuals and communities. It embodies the journey from the past, through the present, and into the future, serving as a source of inspiration, resilience, and cultural continuity.

Kiswahili-Tanzania/Kenya
Mandhari- Scenery, Appearance, View, Landscape, Ambience, Jaunt.

Mandhari inarejelea sifa za kimwili, asili, na kitamaduni. Mazingira ya Kiafrika yamefungamana sana na historia na utamaduni wa binadamu. Pia inaitwa "mama land" inarejelea nchi ya mtu, ardhi ya mababu, au ardhi ambayo ina umuhimu wa kitamaduni na kihisia. Inawakilisha muunganisho wa kina kwa mizizi, mila, na utambulisho wa mtu. Mazingira yanajumuisha hisia pana ya kumilikiwa na urithi wa kitamaduni unaohusishwa na ardhi. Inawakilisha muunganisho wa urithi wa mtu, hisia ya kuhusika, na nanga ya kitamaduni inayounda watu binafsi na jamii. Inajumuisha safari kutoka zamani, kupitia sasa, na katika siku zijazo, ikitumika kama chanzo cha msukumo, uthabiti, na mwendelezo wa kitamaduni.

Runyankole-Uganda
Landscape As Obuteeka, A Reference To The Orderly Arrangement Of Things Culturally - As Nature Should Intend To Have Them In An Uninterferred Setting To Mean Buri Kimwe Kiri Omu Buteeka Bwakyo. Common As Identity Sounds.

Obuteeka ni obumanyiso omu by'obuhangwa, ebirikureebwa hamwe n'eby'enzaarwa.

Obuteeka bw'Ekifirika bwine akakwate kahango n'ebyafaayo hamwe n'eby'enzaarwa

by'abantu. Kandi obundi ekirikwetwa "ensi nyamuzaire", nikimanyisa obutaka

bw'omuntu, ensi ya ba tantenkuru ningashi ensi eine amakuru maingi ahaby'enzaarwa n'ebirikutsika enteekateeka. Obuteeka nibworeka akakwate kahango akariho aha

bukomooko bw'omuntu, emitwarize hamwe n'ahu arikubarirwa. Obuteeka burimu

okutwariza hamwe ahu omuntu arikubarirwa hamwe n'obugaiga bw'eby'enzaarwa

ebikwatiraine n'ensi. Nibworeka akakwate akariho n'eby'enzaarwa ahu turikubarirwa n'obuhamizo bw'enzaarwa ebirikubumba omuntu na bagyenzi be. Obuteeka burimu

orugyendo kuruga ahu turugire, kuraba ahu turi, kandi n'ahu turikuza; obwo biri enshuro y'omuhimbo, okwangisiriza hamwe n'obuhangaazi bw'eby'enzaarwa.

Kinywarwanda-Rwanda
Ibyiza Nyaburanga- Natural Beauty

Ibyiza nyaburanga bigizwe n'uburanga karemano,ibidukikije ndetse n'umuco.Ibyiza nyaburanga by'afurika bisobetse amateka ya muntu n'umuco. Aribyo byitwa" Ubutaka bwa mama" bisobanuye Ubutaka bwanjye,Ubutaka bw'abakurambere cyangwa Ubutaka bubitse igisobanuro cy'umuco n'amarangamutima. Birasobanura isano ry'imbitse ry'inkomoko ya muntu,uruhererekane rw'imico,n',ibirango byawo. Ibyiza nyaburanga bigizwe no kumva haraho ubarizwa, umurage w'umuco ugizwe n'ubutaka.

Ibyiza nyaburanga bigaragaza isano ry'umurage wo kugira Aho ubarizwa n'umuco nk'ingabo igize muntu ndetse naho abarizwa. Ibyiza nyaburanga bibumbatie urugendo rwahahise,rugaragaza none ndetse nejo hazaza.Bigaragaza Kandi isoko y'imyumvire yo kwigira no guharanira k'umuco uramba.

Zanzibar is a typical old coastal town in Tanzania, representing the remnants of the colonial era. This historical town carries the charm and character of its past, with its architecture, narrow streets, and cultural heritage reflecting the influence of various cultures, including Arab, Persian, Indian, and European. The meeting of the old and new in Zanzibar could signify the preservation of cultural traditions and historical landmarks amidst the changing times. It suggests a potential future where historical sites are valued and integrated into modern development, promoting cultural tourism and sustainable growth.

Kampala, the capital city of Uganda, represents present urban development in East Africa. As a bustling metropolis, it showcases the rapid growth, infrastructure advancements, and urbanization that have occurred in recent years. The fusion of the old and new in Kampala could symbolize the challenges and opportunities associated with urban development, such as preserving historical landmarks while embracing modernity. It highlights the importance of sustainable urban planning, infrastructure development, and social progress in shaping the future of cities in the region.

Musanze, a rural town in Rwanda, represents the future landscapes of East Africa with its lush vegetation and natural beauty. Rwanda, known for its environmental initiatives and conservation efforts, demonstrates a vision of sustainable development. The juxtaposition of the old and new in Musanze could imply a future where ecological preservation and sustainable practices are at the forefront of development. It suggests a potential future where rural areas thrive through eco-tourism, sustainable agriculture, and a harmonious coexistence with nature.

Burundi Tunes Mama, a song by Khadja Nin, is featured in the video (*video was showcased at The Moving African Landscape Exhibition in Venice, Italy 2023*) .

The song "Mama" by Burundian musician Khadja Nin carries a powerful message that resonates with the connection between landscape, culture, and the enduring spirit of a people. The lyrics "your spirit never dies" can be interpreted as a reflection of the resilience, strength, and longevity of both the African landscape and its rich cultural heritage. the lyrics "your spirit never dies" can be seen as a testament to the resilience of African cultures and their ability to adapt and evolve while still maintaining a strong connection to their roots. Khadja Nin oWen sings in Swahili, Kirundi and French. A strong connection to her roots, a spirit that lives on.

Overall, the concept of the old meeting the new in these East African countries signifies a dynamic future where the preservation of historical and cultural heritage, sustainable urban development, and ecological conservation intersect. It highlights the need for responsible and inclusive approaches to development that honor the past while embracing progress, ultimately shaping a promising future for the region.

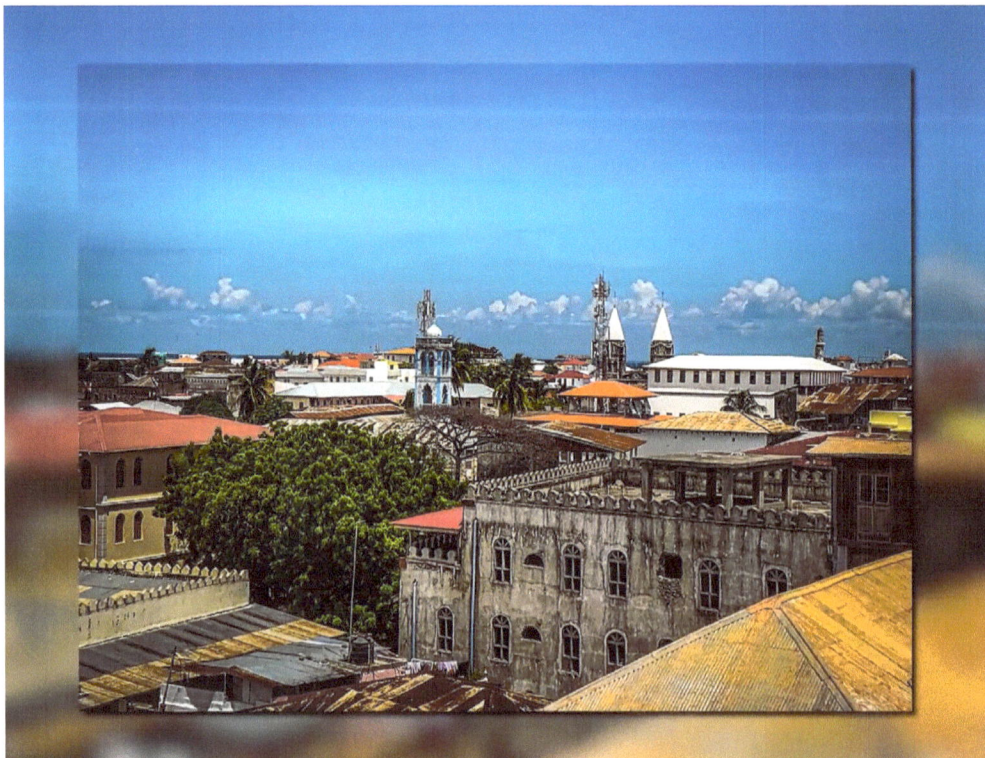

IMAGES DESCRIPTION

ZANZIBAR

01. The Stone Town of Zanzibar, represents a remarkable fusion of diverse cultural influences from Africa, the Arab region, India, and Europe, creating a distinct and unique culture. While it served as a significant center for the slave trade in acquiring and trading slaves from mainland Africa with the Middle East, Stone Town also has great symbolic importance in the suppression of slavery, where campaigns against slavery were orchestrated.

02. The Old Fort, also known as "Ngome Kongwe" in Swahili, is a solid stone fortress located adjacent to the House of Wonders in Zanzibar. Built in the 17th century by the Omanis.

03. Zanzibar's beaches offer a perfect blend of relaxation, adventure, and natural beauty, making them sought-aXer des5na5ons for beach lovers and water enthusiasts. A picturesque stretch of coastline.

KAMPALA

01. Kampala Road is one of the main arterial roads in the heart of Kampala, the capital city of Uganda. It is a bustling and vibrant street that serves as a major commercial and business hub.

02. Uganda House: Uganda House holds historical significance and boasts a remarkable architectural design that blends and marks a shift from traditional to modern elements. Built in 1980, over the years, it has become an iconic symbol of Kampala's urban landscape.

MUSANZE

01. Diana Fossey Campus seamlessly blends with its natural environment and employs locally obtained materials. A commitment to conservation and minimizing environmental impact, demonstrating a strong dedication to conservation and minimizing environmental footprint.

02. Virunga Mountains provide a breathtaking backdrop of lush greenery and towering peaks. The mountains offer opportunities for hiking, volcano climbing (including Mount Karisimbi and Mount Bisoke), and nature walks, allowing visitors to immerse themselves in the region's stunning landscapes.

CHAPTER 4

EXPLORING URBAN AFRICA

Bukunmi Oyewole
Photographer
Ibadan, Nigeria

YORUBA:

Ala ile se pataki simi nitoripe oni ewa iseda olohun ni agbaye. Won nfa oun afojiri ati ifokanbale, tin somipo mo awon oun iyanu ti aye yi. Ala ile nsise irani leti aye wa laarin aworan nla aye wa, osi tun se iwuri ijinle imoriri fun iseda aye yi. Nwon funni itunu, ibi irisi, ati orisun awokose, toun ranmi leti isopo aye yi. Ala ile je ferese si orisirisi ayika, asa, ati itan, tin'sawari ati iwuri iyanu aye ti an'gbe.

Landscapes are very important to me because they contain the beauty of our natural world. They evoke a sense of admiration and tranquility, connecting me to the wonders of the Earth. Landscapes serve as a reminder of our place within a larger backdrop of life and inspire a deep appreciation for nature's design. They offer solace, a place to reflect, and a source of inspiration, reminding me of the connectivity of our planet. Landscapes are windows into different environments, cultures, and histories, inviting exploration and encouraging a sense of wonder for the world we inhabit.

The African landscape according to my pictures refers to the visual and physical characteristics of an urban environment. It encompasses the arrangement and appearance of buildings, infrastructure, streets, parks, and other elements that shape the overall aesthetic and functionality of a city. City landscapes often reflect the architectural styles, cultural influences, and development patterns of a particular urban area, showcasing a blend of human-made structures and natural surroundings. The city landscape serves as a dynamic platform for cultural expression, where art, fashion, cuisine, and literature flourish, showcasing the creativity and resilience of African communities. It is a testament to the spirit of innovation and the fusion of tradition and modernity that defines African urban life.

CHAPTER 5

KUNGODA

Tiécoura N'Daou
Visual Artist
Bamako, Mali

In the Bambara language of Mali, the expression that comes close to the word landscape is called "KUNGODA". It is not certain that there is a word or words in the languages spoken in Mali that would correspond to what we understand by landscape in the Occident.

The expression Kungoda therefore refers to nature and the environment. It is cosmic and mythical. But the term landscape in Occident culture is mainly visual.

In my photographic approaches of landscape, I capture a moment of life. I try to make the viewer relive this magical moment that I felt.

CHAPTER 6

THE SANKOFA

Tyler M. Littles is a 2023 Graduate of Tuskegee Universities Architecture program from Montgomery Alabama. Tyler has a passion for design story telling, community focused architecture, and historic preservation. He is soon to commence a position as a design architect with Perkins + Will in June.

Professor Amma Asamoah is a daughter of the Diaspora and Ghana who has a passion for bridging the ancestral cousins through her courses and the AwukuBa Foundation, her non profit . A mother of four she is a also full time professor of architecture, sustainable designer and researcher at her Alma Matter Tuskegee University. Professor Asamoah will begin her Doctoral Studics at Carnegie Mellon University in the Fall.

Weija, Ghana

The dispersal of African people all over the globe has caused major shifts in the African Architectural Landscape. More than four centuries ago the forced removal of millions of Africans from their homeland through the trans-Atlantic slave trade robbed the African continent of much of its intellectual prowess and labor force. Thus, the continent's infrastructural and economic development was stifled by centuries of subjugation and enslavement under colonial rule. The architectural knowledge deeply rooted in a connection with culture, ancestry, and the natural environment was buried and replaced by brutal concrete forts.

This design solution was developed by Tyler Littles a recent graduate of "Tuskegee Universities Robert R. Taylor School of Architecture and Construction science. "The Sankofa" is responding to the call for an architectural language that reconnects repatriates, returning to Ghana to commemorate the year of return to their ancestral homeland.

The architectural landscape is cited in Weija Ghana a suburb 20 miles west of the capital city of Accra on land inherited by professor Amma Asamoah. Tyler explored the form and meaning behind the Baobab tree and the Sacred Adinkra symbol of Sankofa.

Concept : The tree in African cultures can represent our connection between heaven and Earth. It also represents our ties to family and ancestry. It's value is infinite as it provides oxygen to breathe, fruits to nurture us, shade as protection and the strength in its trunk and roots

The Baobab tree in its many forms has been a revered species throughout the African continent for centuries it has served as a place for gathering, learning and in some cases living in the African landscape.

Tyler choose to investigate three species of the sacred Baobab and how its form could be translated into a sustainable community for African diasporan's to live, gather, and learn. The residential complex draws inspiration from the functions of the three species, Gregori, Granderii and the Za. The design modernizes the traditional building material of rammed earth while integrating renewable energy and green storm water infrastructure on the site. The name of the complex "Sankofa, go back and take it" represents the reclaiming of our ancestral knowledge. The design is meant to reject Western colonial standards and celebrate built forms rooted in African heritage.

Context Map

THE GREGORII
715 SQ FT PER UNIT

2 Bedroom
2 Bathroom
Kitchen
Patio

THE GRANDERII
427 SQ FT PER UNIT

1 Bedroom
1 Bathroom
Kitchen
Patio

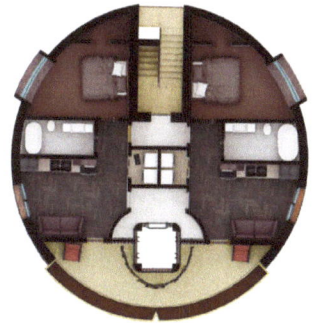

THE ZA
1,035 SQ FT PER UNIT

3 Bedroom
2 Bathroom
Kitchen
Patio

SUSTAINABILTY DIAGRAM

Passive Cooling

This design acheives passive cooling through techniques such as windows operable. the use of trees plants. and natural wind. Buildings perform like tree funneling the air-flow and cooling the central space.

Green Roofing

Like the crown of a tree. the green function as way to harvest and minimize the buildup of rainwater on flat roofs. Roofing will retain up to 60% of rainwater and return back to building as greywater.

Energy

The design of building has incorparate two ways of pro-ducinh self-suffient energy. wind turbines and solar pan-els. The combination of these two methods will help to offset the cost of electricy and provide backup power in case infustruture failure.

Rainwater Management

Using of the advantage of a sloping topography, the site features two retention ponds at the bottom of site to collect rainwater. Rainwater would be filtered back in the building as greywater.

The site also utilizes permable to as welll to limit water build-up on walking paths.

KEY

Secondary Wind
Primary Wind
Harmattan Wind
Greenery

SOUTH ELEVATION

CHAPTER 7

POSTCARDS

Alice Christel PENDA aka AWA
Visual Artist, Art Teacher
Yaounde, Cameroon

Définition Paysage Africain (French): Ma perception visuelle de l'Afrique dans laquelle je vis.

African landscape definition (English): It's my personal visual perception of the Africa I inhabit.

Design concept and cultural overview:

I designed a set of postcards, representing my country's landscapes. These allegories depict the Republic of Cameroon as a large slaves' plantation (banana republic).

On top of highest hills, the Central Bank (BEAC) building and the country's presidency are recognizable. Just below, we see cash crop plantations; and, in the valley, miserable peasant's houses.

The postcards are made accordingly to XAF currency bank notes' proportions and colors. This choice aims at showing Cameroonian landscape is shaped by the country's economic system.

My pictures enlighten a phenomena invisible to the eye and untold; a hidden truth.

For instance, "Cameroon-Kamerun" is a plantation project envisioned by 19th century's German settlers. It was about cutting a piece of Central Africa territory; and, exploiting its lands and indigenous inhabitants to grow cash crops for Europe. It has been launched in 1884, by the ratification of a treaty between German merchants and indigenous leaders. France took over the project by the sake of WWI.

Surprisingly, 60 years after the independence proclamation, exogenous agro-industries are still dictating their iniquitous law. Local populations and lands are still abusively exploited to feed Europe. This "slavery in disguise" capitalistic mode is pursued with government's complicity. 140 years after its launch, "Kamerun" project is a "success". Although, none of the initial stakeholders benefit from it anymore. Indeed, 80% of Cameroonian are victimized by it, for France's profit.

These artworks aim at expressing, Cameroonians problem is rooted in Cameroon DNA. From the beginning, it was; and, still is an enslaving plantation.

This work is a testimony of the present tense; a claim aiming at opening suffering populations' eyes; and, a proposition of starting point to find appropriate solutions that will definitely free us from colonialism's burden.

Paradoxically, these illustrations depicting institutionalized injustice, appear to be relaxing. Plus, the landscapes seems worth visiting; or, staying. The postcards are, somehow, carrying Africa's mood-soul; that is, a hellish paradise / paradisiac hell...

« Papaya Republic Landscape», Alice PENDA, 2023, 840 × 420 cm

« Cotton Republic Landscape » , Alice PENDA, 840 × 420 cm

CHAPTER 8

ABIYAMỌ, THE PROTECTOR OF MY CHILDREN!

Olubunmi Tayo Agboola (PhD) is an African ecofeminist who revers and tends to Mother Earth,
English Department,
Ajayi Crowther University, Oyo, Nigeria

I AM A WOMAN! I AM ABIYAMỌ, THE PROTECTOR OF MY CHILDREN!

Olumo-rock, the abiyamọ, sits on a vast expanse of land in splendour and dignity, a great fortress wall that had protected and hidden the Egba people from external enemies. Many have suggested that Olumo-rock is masculine because it is a rock, a belief that is ingrained in the Yoruba cosmological worldview. However, images of the rock have revealed that it is a pregnant woman praying for and enclosing her offspring. Olumo's structure is that of a pregnant woman lying down. The Iroko tree represents the leg, the middle of the stomach, the protruded part of the breast, and the upper part of the neck. The head is on the other side. Olumo is the structure of a pregnant woman! Her pregnancy reveals her fertility- a carrier and protector of life. As a result, it is not surprising that Olumo-rock served as a haven for the Egbas during their three-year war with the Dahomey tribe. Abiyamọ, a true mother, demonstrates feminine characteristics such as love, care, and compassion in her motherly role of preserving the ecosystem and human entities in her vicinity.

I AM A WOMAN! I AM WURA, ADORE ME!

Abiyamọ is Wura. A priceless precious gem Olumo-rock, decked out in feminine regalia, is a mother worth far more than rubies, deserving of adoration and worship. Wura is worshipped in a specific location known as Ojubo-Olumo. No one can share Wura's glory. She lives in her temple, and her entrance is adorned with white welcoming her children who have come to pray and give thanks. As a ritual procedure, Wura accepts a black cow with no spots, bitter kola, kola nut, pigeon, and guinea fowl. Avoiding worshipping Wura disrupts the natural chain of being, which has tangible consequences. Wura is Abiyamọ, and Abiyamọ is the guiding angel of her children.

Side view of Abiyamo, Olumo Rock, July 2022. Source: O.T. Agboola

The place were Egbas hid during the Egba & Dahomey Intertribal War, 1830-1833, under the Olumo Rock, July 2022.
Source: O.T. Agboola

Entrance into the rock-rooms, where the Egbas hid, Olumo Rock, July 2022. Source: O.T. Agboola

One of the entrances into the rooms where the indigenes lived under the rock, Olumo Rock, July 2022.
Source: O.T. Agboola.

CHAPTER 9

AN AFRICAN LENS ON THE TERM "LANDSCAPES"

Opaluwa Ejiga (Phd),
Department of Architecture,
Afe Babalola University Ado-Ekiti, Nigeria

Diverse groups now have diverse meanings when they use the term "landscape."

Most fields have adopted the term "landscape," as shown in words like "architectural landscape," "political landscape," "cultural landscape," "economic landscape," and others. I would define the term landscape as an expanse of space that inherits the sensual and aesthetic characteristics of the elements within its field and allows users to see forms, hear sounds, feel and perceive the various interactions among the constituent elements and themselves. Simply put landscape is an expanse of space that takes on the sensory and aesthetic qualities of the objects in its vicinity and enables users to see shapes, hear noises, experience sensations, and recognise the various connections between the objects and themselves.

Below are images that paint the words that describe the term Landscape but from the African lens:

The Urban Landscape of Kampala, Uganda (2012) Source: Opaluwa Ejiga

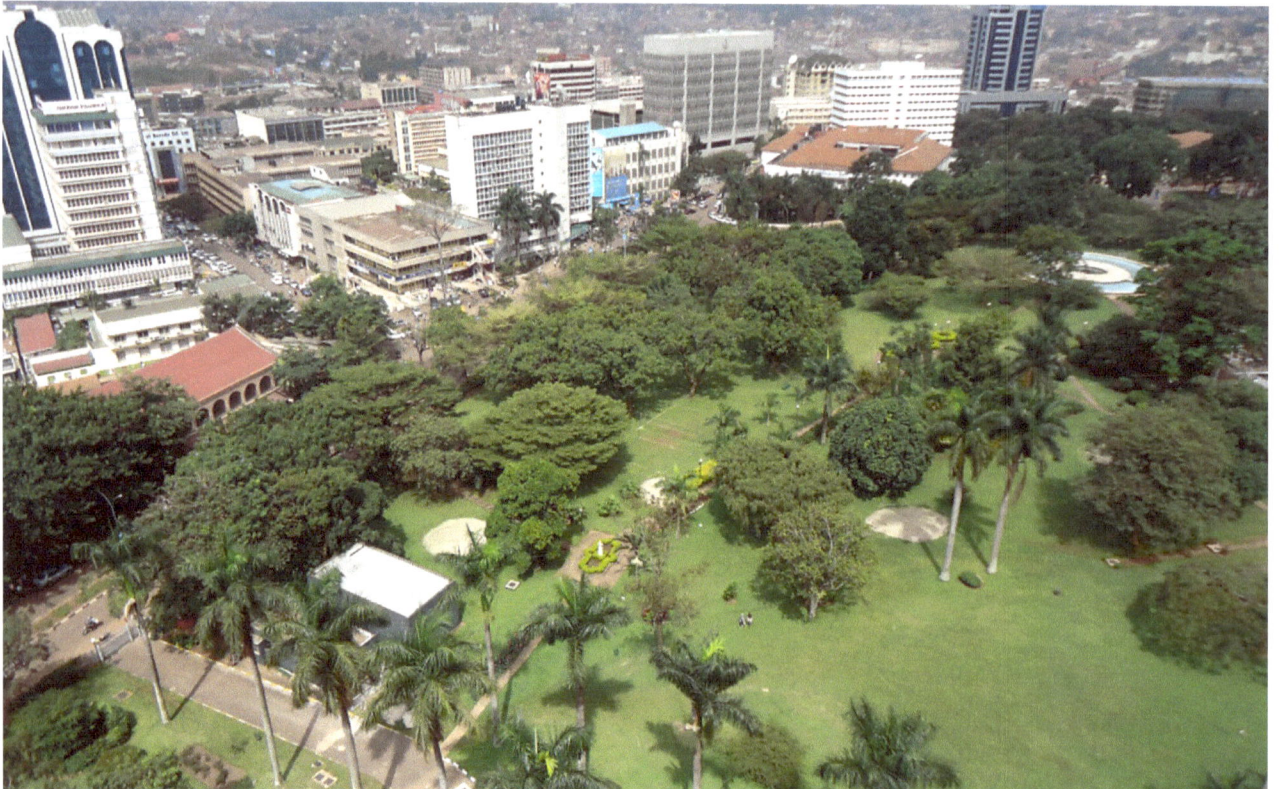

Green Open Space of downtown Kampala, Uganda (2012). Source: Opaluwa Ejiga

Ariel View capturing the Dual City concept (European Quarters vs. Indigenous Peoples' Quarters) of the Urban Landscape of Kampala, Uganda (2012). Source: Opaluwa Ejiga

Rear view of Kajuru Castle - a private owned luxury resort loated in Kajuru, Kaduna State, Nigeria (2014)
Source: Opaluwa Ejiga

Streetscape of Catholic Mission Street showing Holy Cross Cathedral Lagos Island, Nigeria (2014)
Source: Opaluwa Ejiga

Accessible portion of the Nnachaalo River and Oma-Idoko scared grounds Idah, Kogi State, Nigeria (2023)
Source: Opaluwa Ejiga

CHAPTER 10

AFRICAN CULTURAL LANDSCAPES – A CASE OF KOFYAR HILL SETTLEMENT

Dr Obafemi Olukoya,
Brandenburgische Technische Universität Cottbus - Senftenberg
Fakultät 2 - Lehrstuhl Umweltplanung
Kofyar, Nigeria

African cultural landscapes offer alternative worldviews to the prevailing Western ones – usually depicting humans as an integral part of nature instead of being separated from it and trying to dominate it. This is often based on complementarities, correspondences, reciprocities, and varied levels of trialogues. Kofyar hill settlement is a typical example of African organically evolving cultural landscapes which has emerged based on "initial social, economic, administrative, and/or religious imperative and has developed its present form by association with and in response to its natural environment. Such landscapes reflect that process of evolution in their form and component features" (Operational Guideline 2021 paragraph 47, p. 22)

The cultural landscape is located in Qua'an Pan Local Government Area of Plateau State, Nigeria. It is located east of the geographical center of Nigeria, measuring over 30km long by 16km wide, intersected by latitude 9°N and longitude 9°15'E (Netting, 1968; 1993). The boundary of the indigenous hill settlement contains features such as the unique circular stone; stone fort walls which are result of indigenous African fortification techniques; farm terraces constructed using locally available irregular dry stone walls making cultivable land space on the sloppy terrain; unique dry stone animal pens which are testimonies to their megalithic technique; stone paved roads; pyramidal stone graves where the local communities re-establish the mystic bonds between their gods and ancestors.

BIBLIOGRAPHY

Robert Netting (1968). Hill Farmers of Nigeria; Cultural Ecology of the Kofyar of the Jos Plateau. Seattle: University of Washington Press.

Robert Netting (1993). Smallholders, Householders; Farm Families and the Ecology of Intensive, Sustainable Agriculture. Stanford: Stanford University Press.

UNESCO (2021). Operational Guidelines for the Implementation of the World Heritage Convention. Paris.

CHAPTER 11

HOMESTEAD SPATIAL LANDSCAPES

Angelene Clarke
Spatial Syntactician, Spatial Analyst with Beaded Ladies
Ghana

Researchers in environmental psychology, anthropology and architecture have tried to explain the impact of syntonic responses to spatial configurations found throughout the African nations. The organisation of past and future urban space continues to be an important focus of spatial insight and their connection to cultural contexts within African landscapes.

This short review presents some of the underlying theories and ideas and studies influencing the most recent debates and discussions centred on African spatial studies, and the role space syntax theory plays on rebalancing the prevailing cultural perspective of *Moving African Landscapes.*

Typically, spatial landscapes are viewed through a morphic language that constitute rather than represent the social network. For example, Lynch understood the urban landscape through hierarchical order, categorised as paths, edges, districts, nodes, or landmarks, "...patterned together to provide satisfying systematic structure as a coherent pattern" (Lynch, 1960). Similarly Hanson stated that visual perception brings into play the relationship between visibility; what you can see and permeability; where you can go." (Hanson, 1999).

However, this theory does not explicitly explain the spatial and cultural order observed in spatial order such as the palace complex at Gede, Kenya or Tallensi compounds. Where cognitive psychological literature indicates spatial awareness is influenced by other factors, including experience, familiarity, balance, distinction, complexity, and perceptual articulacy.

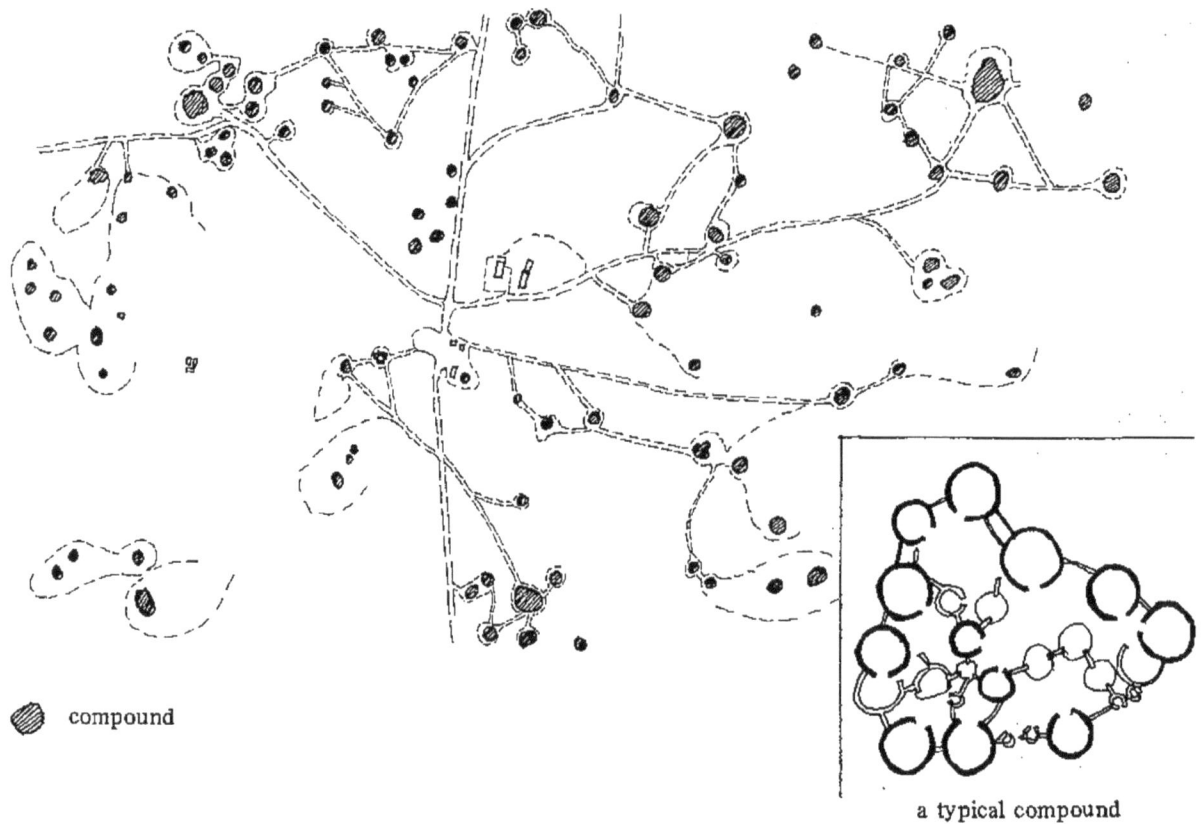

Fig 1: Tongo—A Tallensi settlement, Ghana (Prussin, 1969).

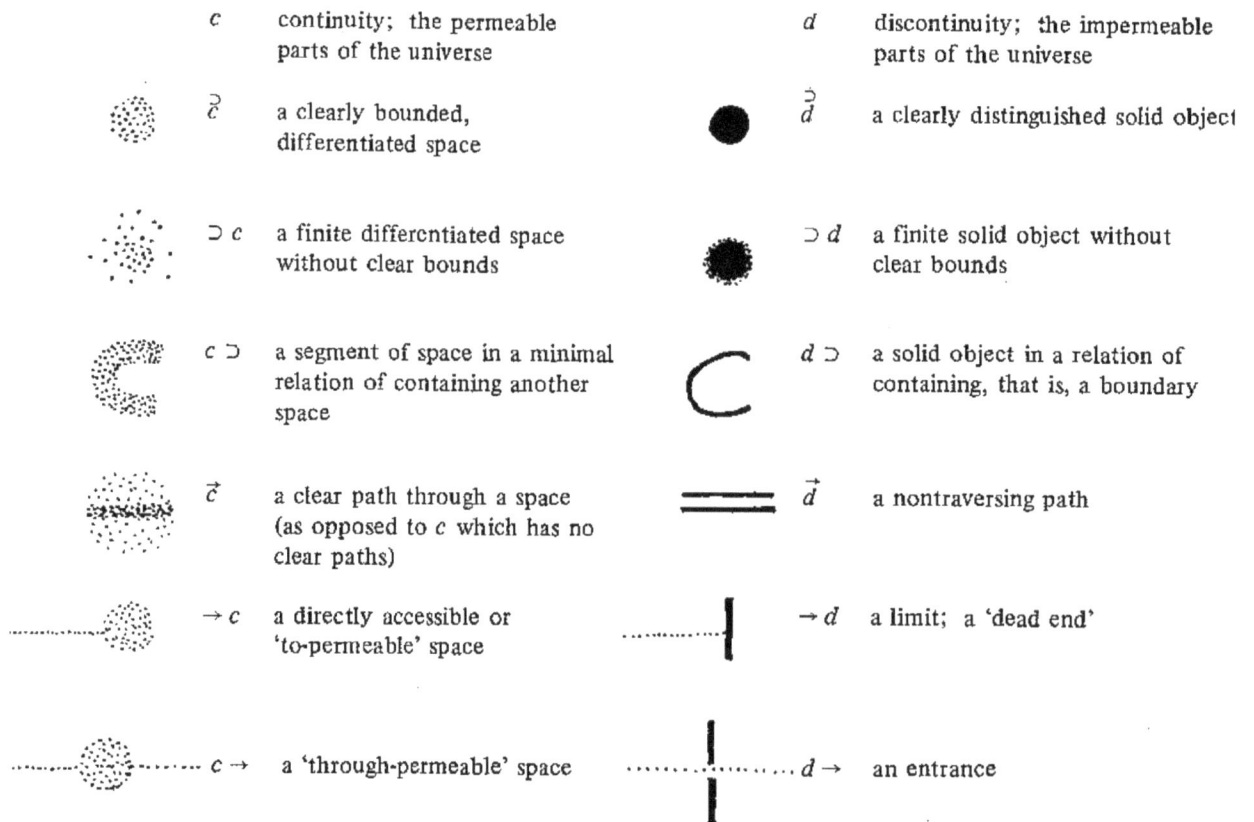

	c	continuity; the permeable parts of the universe		d	discontinuity; the impermeable parts of the universe
	$\overset{\supset}{c}$	a clearly bounded, differentiated space		$\overset{\supset}{d}$	a clearly distinguished solid object
	$\supset c$	a finite differentiated space without clear bounds		$\supset d$	a finite solid object without clear bounds
	$c \supset$	a segment of space in a minimal relation of containing another space		$d \supset$	a solid object in a relation of containing, that is, a boundary
	$\vec{c}$	a clear path through a space (as opposed to c which has no clear paths)		$\vec{d}$	a nontraversing path
	$\to c$	a directly accessible or 'to-permeable' space		$\to d$	a limit; a 'dead end'
	$c \to$	a 'through-permeable' space		$d \to$	an entrance

Fig 2: Elementary lexicon. The diagrams are illustrative rather than rigorous and are included as an aid to understanding the argument (Hiller, 1996).

With space syntax, an analytical approach emphasises maps as sources for understanding space and spatial relationships embedded in built or social forms. The quantitative descriptions of street networks produced by space syntax analyses, formulates, and tests hypotheses about patterns of urban movement, encounters and socio-economic activities from the past that can help in the interpretation of other historical source materials to give an overall account of urban spatial culture.

Space syntax is a set of theories linking space and society and a set of techniques for analysing spatial configuration (Hillier et al, 1983; Hillier and Hanson, 1998). For Hillier 'The origins of relational schemes of space, lie somewhere between the ordering capacities of the mind and the spatial ordering inherent in the ways in which social relationships are realised in space (Hillier, 2004). The key principles of syntactic methods are explained by clarifying the relationship of space syntax to HGIS (Historical Geographical Information Systems and archaeological research). Several academic studies have tried to objectively understand the spatial landscapes observed in African states through experimental investigation.

The analysis of visibility and movement offers insight into African urban structure while also addressing their cultural contexts based on archaeological research. A study by Monika Baumanova (2020) examined the street networks, and the socio-spatial role of urban quarters of the East African coast. This study demonstrated how spatial partitioning and cultural heritage affects sensory perceptions such as vision and kinaesthetics.

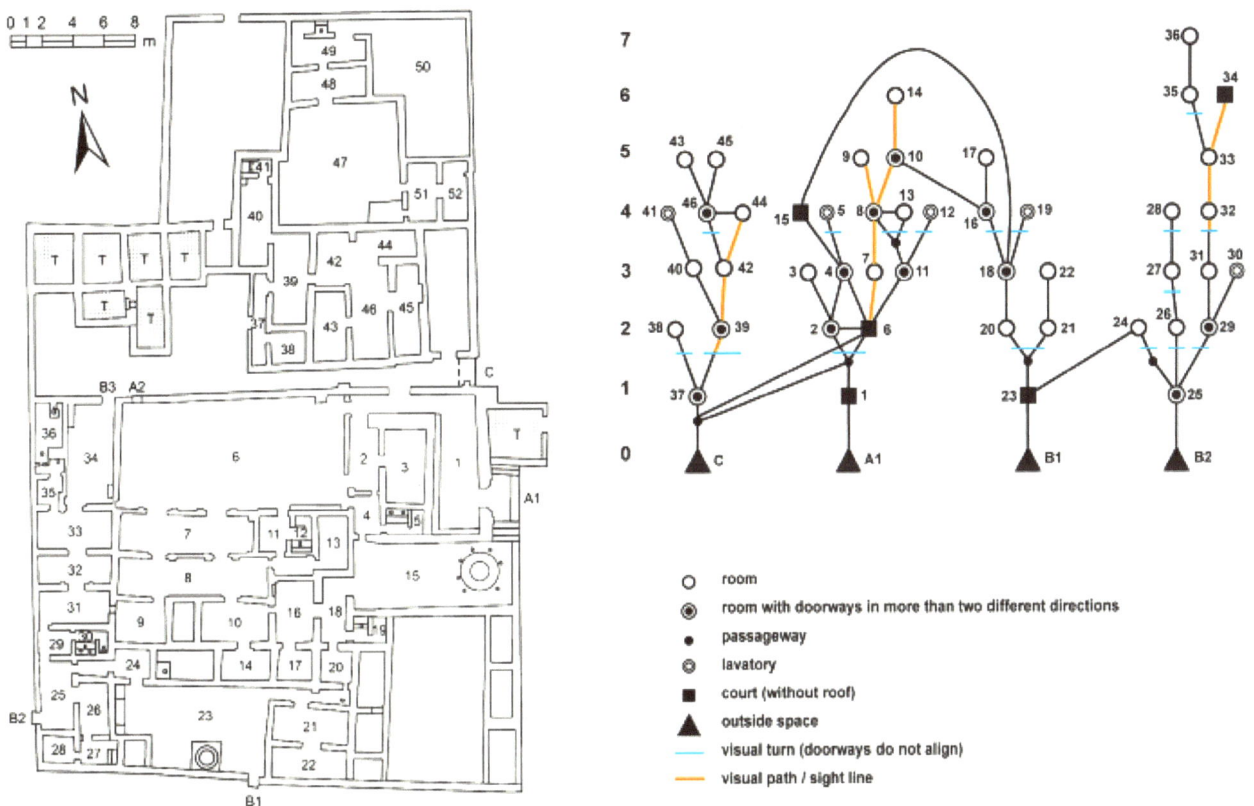

Fig 3: The Palace complex at Gede, Kenya Image shows the integration of small 'house-like' units into the palace structure (Baumanova, 2020).

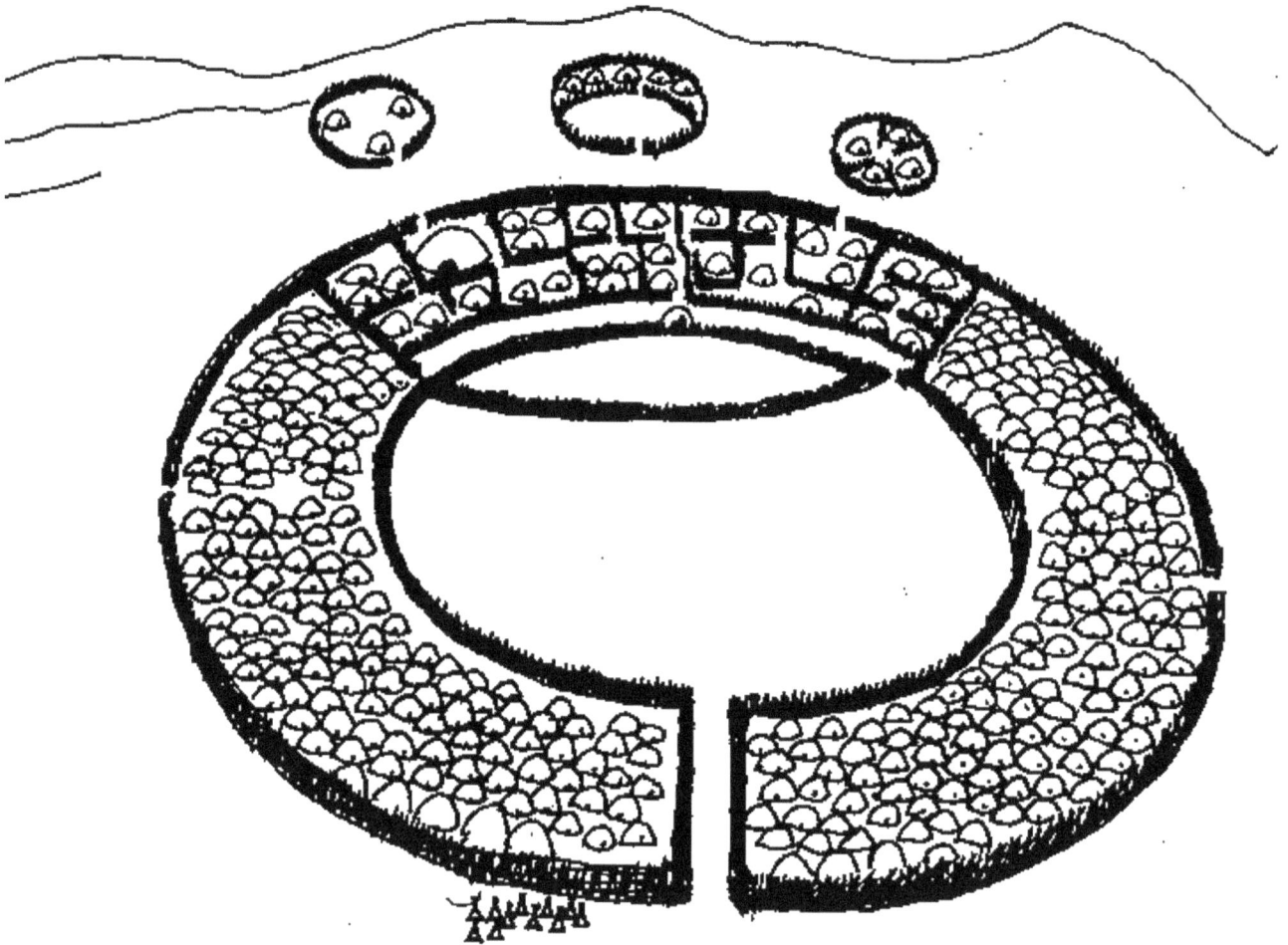

Fig 4: Zulu Royal Kraal (Gluckman, 1960).

Studies by Koranteng, Christian, Barbara Simons and J. Awume investigated the evolution of Spatial Configurations in Ghana's housing sector and the impact of movement in spatial affordance. Researchers identified the increasing negative effects (depression, marginalisation, loneliness) as a culture moved away from communal living, including within the nuclear family structures and spaces. The study provided syntactic scientific evidence of the spatial shift in configuration in the Ghanaian housing sector.

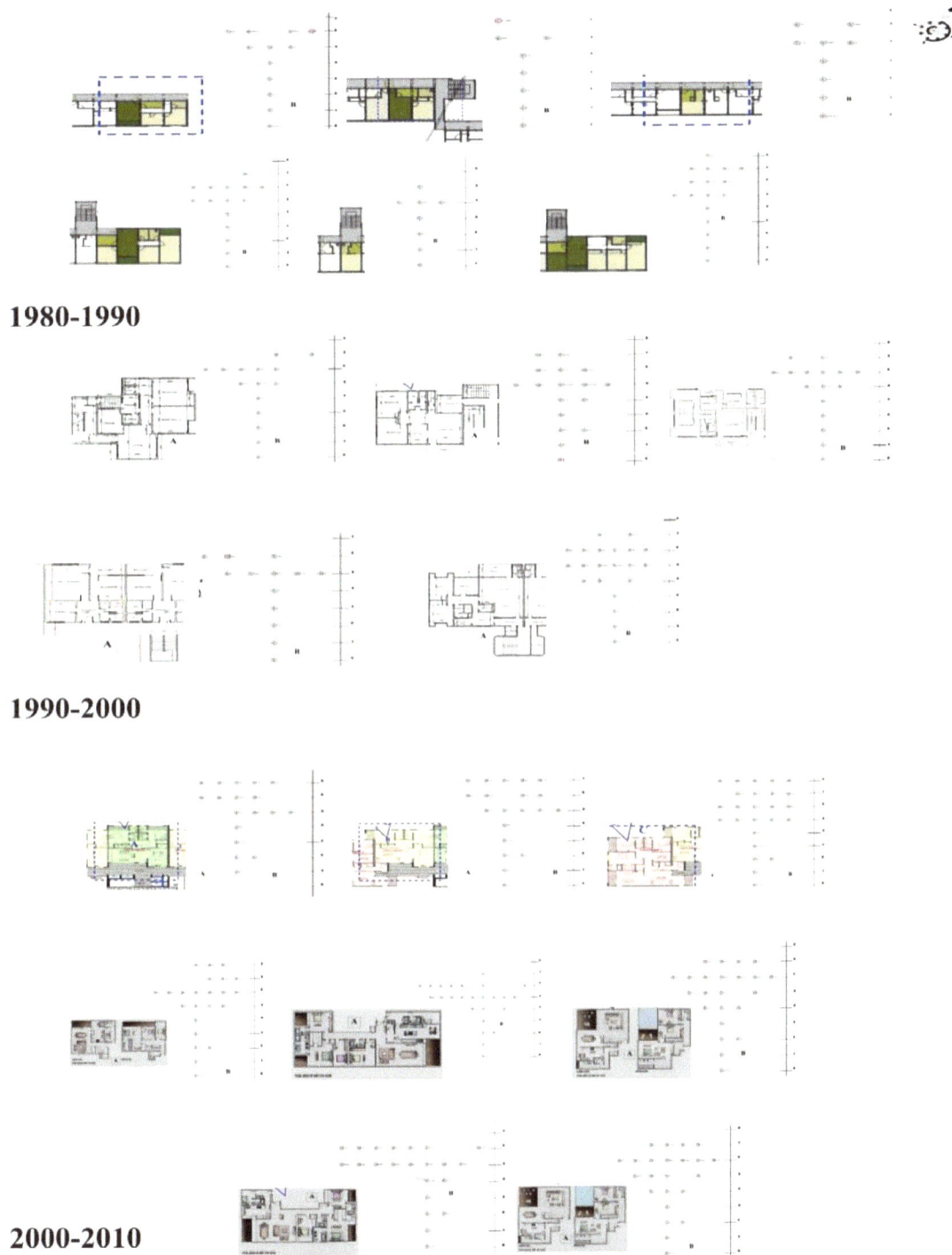

1980-1990

1990-2000

2000-2010

Fig 5: Justified Permeability Graphs (Gamma Maps) of some of the selected Ghanaian spatial configuration layouts (Clarke, 2021).

Julienne Hanson through Decoding Homes and Houses (1999) introduces syntactic techniques designed to retrieve and interpret the social and symbolic coding embedded in spatial structure. Her analysis, representations and measures show how archaeologic domestic space provided a framework for everyday life. Furthermore, she demonstrated how social meanings are constructed in the home and how different sub-groups within society differentiate themselves through their patterns of domestic space and lifestyles, her evidence shows how spatial order has shifted in landscapes of the past to those observed at present.

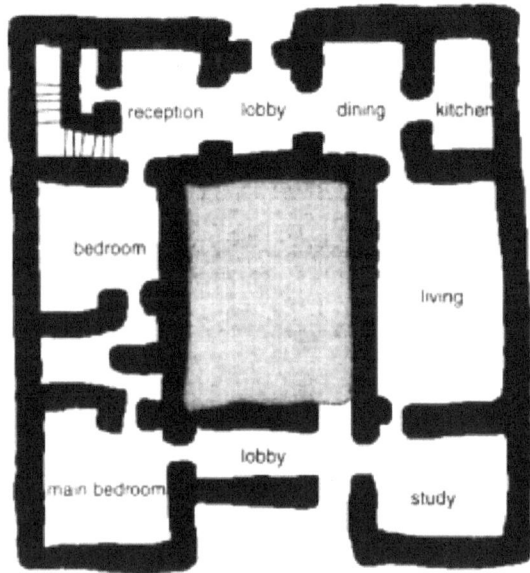

George Schwindwoski, Berlin

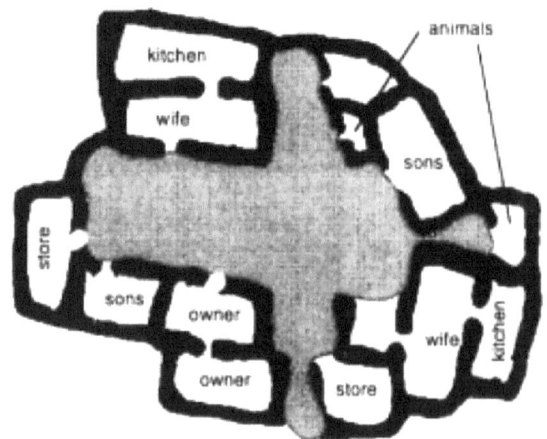

Isala house, Sekai, Ghana

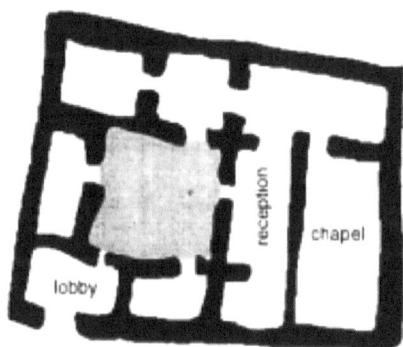

Sumerian house, Ur

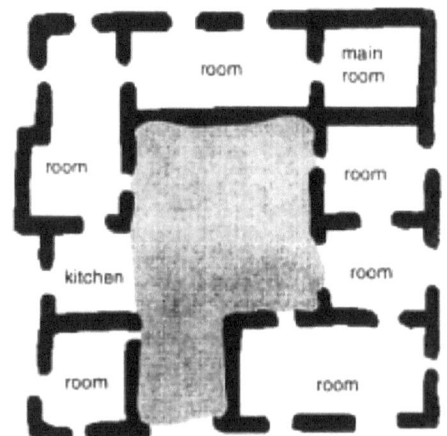

Korean house, An Dong

Fig 6: Four comparative courtyard houses from the historical record in four countries (Hanson,1999).

Figure 1.14

Plans and justified graphs of the Tallensi compounds

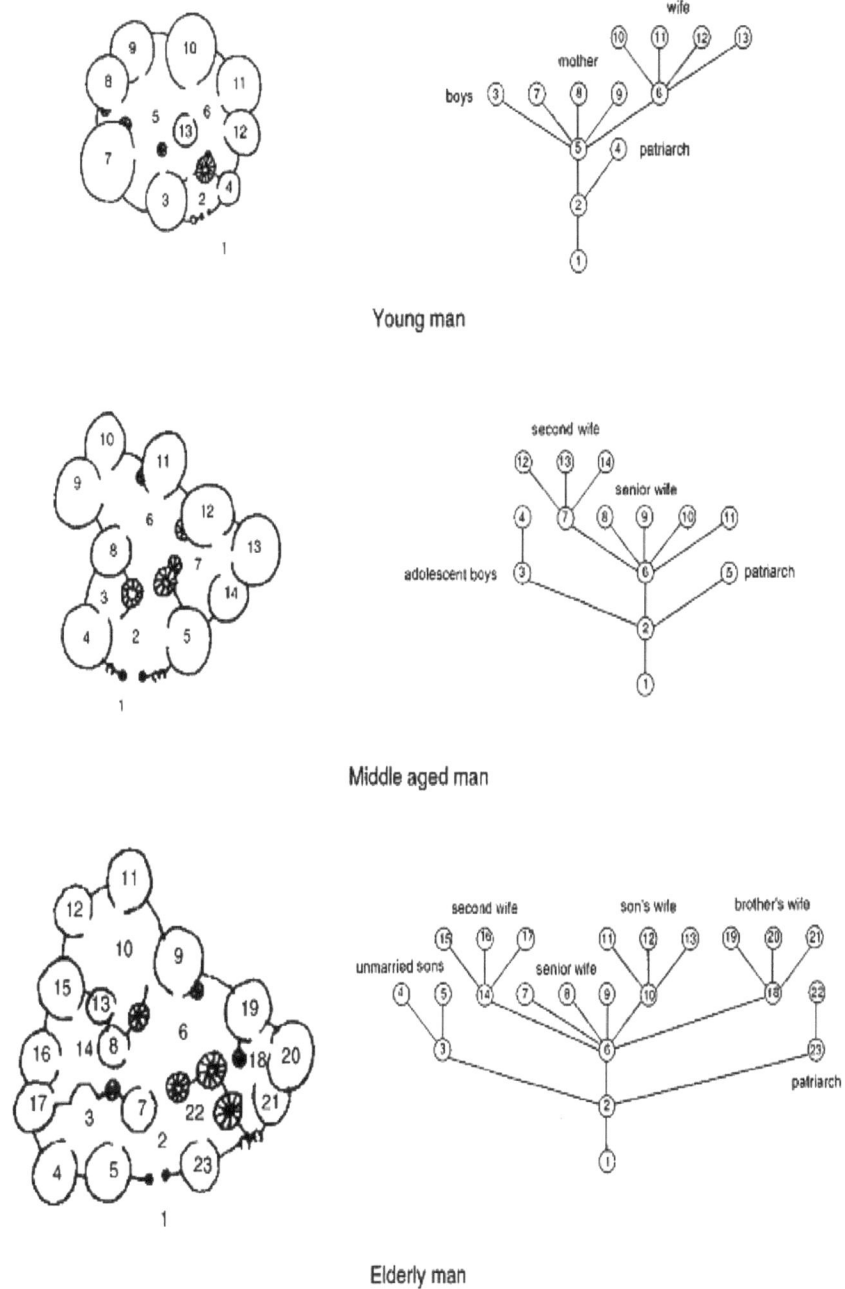

Young man

Middle aged man

Elderly man

Fig 7: Tallensi Compound (Prussin, 1969).

Hanson's study of the compounds of the Tallensi of Northern Ghana, through the depicted process of Fortes in the 1940s and 1950s and by Prussin in the 1960s revealed that the basic, irreducible physical interface of Tallensi society is the homestead, a compound made up of simple, circular, mud-built huts with thatched roofs joined together by a perimeter wall. The space in the vicinity of the entrance is marked by a boabab or 'shade' tree, and ancestor shrines. For Hanson the configurational analysis of the floor plans and spatial network is conceived of as an 'archaeology of space capturing the pattern of invariance in inhabitant-inhabitant and inhabitant-visitor relations. Which in this case very functional patterned landscape defined.

'For the Tallensi, the senior wife's courtyard and her suite of rooms are strategically located at the branching point of the trunk. She controls access to the courtyards of more junior wives, who share a milliet grinding room.'

From Hanson's study to Koranteng's investigations, using syntax techniques clearly to identify the shifting phenomenon in the spatial and cultural landscape allows researchers to examine the relationship between spatial configuration through the evaluation *order, complexity, openness as metrics.* Building on Hillier's theory of order, structure, and theory of natural movement (Hillier et al., 1993a) utilises geospatial, syntactic and empirical methods, to examine users' behavioural response to the immediate, will allow the next wave of researchers to question what factors determines Africa's next spatial landscape move.

BIBLIOGRAPHY

Koranteng, C., Simons, B. and Awume, J.(2019). Evolution of Spatial Configurations in Ghana's Housing Development: The Case of Private Apartment Buildings in Ghana.

Baumanova, M. (2020). Sensory Synaesthesia: Combined Analyses Based on Space Syntax in African Urban Contexts. Afr Archaeol Rev 37, 125–141. https://doi.org/10.1007/s10437-020-09368-9

Baumanova, M., Smejda, L., & Rüther, H. (2019). Pre-colonial origins of urban spaces in the west African Sahel: Street networks, trade, and spatial plurality. *Journal of Urban History, 45*, 500–516.

Donley-Reid, L. (1987). Life in the Swahili town house reveals the symbolic meaning of spaces and artefact assemblages. *African Archaeological Review, 5*, 181–192.

Prussin, L., (1969). Architecture in Northern Ghana. *University of California Press.*

Hanson, J. (1998). Decoding homes and houses.

Hillier, B. (1996). Space is the Machine: A Configurational Theory of Architecture. *Cambridge University Press.*

Hillier B, Hanson J, Peponis J, Hudson J, & Burdett R. (1983). Space syntax, a different urban perspective. *Architects' Journal , 178*, 47–63.

CHAPTER 12

MAMBAAH KADAI !!!!

This means genuine welcome in the Gbagyi language of the middle belt of Nigeria.

African Moving Landscapes: *The African Vibe is a state of being : connecting the fluidity of African vibe+place+people*

Diana Gbefwi-Guyit, Green Architect
DG Green Foundation.
Regenerative Green Consultant and Founder of DG Green Foundation. Passionate about telling the African story, its landscape, architecture and culture from our lenses.

Maigaskiya Studios,
Photography. Landscape and architectural photography from all around the world, Abuja Nigeria.

'Mambaah kadi, mambaah jesun, mambaah hénhén'.

This is the continuous sounds that you hear as you walk along the paths in a Gbagyi district, the people welcome each other as the ask about welfare, family and wellbeing of they're neighbors. It is part of an unending greeting that holds the community together.

In a bid to understanding the architectural and natural landscapes of Africa's rural, urban and sub urban dwelling, I was led to seek to understand my surroundings from my experience within my place in the community.I asked my self questions as to how our landscapes were formed, how I felt about different places at different times within Nigeria and outside it. I embraced my totality and expressed with words the experience within different landscapes in Nigeria.

First a little story about what inspired my love for landscapes: I always loved visiting my grand mother in the village every Christmas because of the food and the fact that everyone was always around to celebrate together, there were lots of sweet treats and drinks as my grand mother traded honey as a business. My grand father on the other hand had few words, but his few words were always filled with so much wisdom, we did not always see him much during the day but mostly in the evening when he was back from the farm, underneath his feet were so thick as he never believed in putting on shoes, he felt it separated him from his land, he would always walk the dirt paths covered in dandelions and popiseed flowers with his plastic shoes tied around his neck saying shoes always slowed him down, he did not grow up wearing shoes.

- CONNECTION TO EARTH

Growing up I thought that was odd. However, as I grew up I realized the connection we humans have to the earth as it has a continuous

- PERSEVERANCE

Electromagnetic cycle that recharges our body. The more questions I asked, the more experiences came my way. Our landscapes formed organically out of the functions and activities of the dwellings around.

- CONTENTMENT

- ORGANIC WAY OF LIFE

Our landscapes mould us, they are the paths we walk on every day as we touch the ground, they are the sights we see as we come from the market or go to school the are visually imprinted in our subconscious.

- SOUNDS

They are the sounds we hear during the owambe and durbar ceremonies.

The drums that move our hips, legs and hands to its rhythm, the sounds that set our spirits free and connects us with our ancestors forging stronger bonds for us, we dwell in this melodies as our nostrils pick up the habanero, bay leaves and bell pepper aromas coming from the jellof rice and deep fried beef our neighbors are cooking, I find myself ready for a friendly visit because I know a plate will always welcome me at the table.

- FREEDOM OF EXPRESSION

- COMMUNITY

Our landscapes shape our experiences, deepen our values, creates relationships and most of all unites the African communities.

- FLAMBOYANCE

The African way of life can be adopted by any race in any country, it has no boundary, it is rich in deep hues of colours, flamboyant and a bit nosy. It has an expression of organic living, more biophilic than minimalist.

- POWER

The Nigerian landscape lends itself to the simplicities of the rural community as well as the complexity of the urban cities. its a juxtapose of affluence, power and community.

- ANIMALS AS PART OF OUR LANDSCAPES

Our natural landscapes are fluid and flow with ease. On the other hand built up spaces are designed to encourage interaction and dialogue across all age ranges. We stay united by the vibe of the city, our wealth lies directly beneath our feet within our natural resources,

CHAPTER 13

THE LOBI VESSEL

Richard Adetokunbo Aina

The African landscape is a predominantly natural environment, it is the primordial nexus from which all things are birthed. From the earth comes the flora that in turn fuels the fauna which comprises the cyclical oscillations of ecosystems and habitats. Within the interacting movements of these complimentary life forms and opposing forces, the landscape is uniquely shaped by its many cultures and communities. Be it of adobe, cob, banco, rammed earth, earth bricks or wattle and daub, a mix to mold the dwelling encapsulating a people, it is also a host for the consequent ruin and a loved one's burial. Essentially, the earth that is the landscape perpetually ingests and renews.

Approximately 90% to 95% of all sub-Saharan cultural artefacts are housed outside sub-Saharan Africa, according to the 2007 UNESCO forum. A decade later at the University of Ouagadougou, President Macron in a seminal speech – vowed that France would begin to return West African objects of antiquity that are in their possession. Located in traditional Lobi land, the vessel is introduced as a traditionally infused contemporary vernacular earthen architecture for the Lobi peoples that rehouses and spiritually rehabilitates their bateba figures of antiquity. Four consistently key and prominent figures within traditional Lobi culture are identified, being the master masons, craftsmen, diviners and land chiefs. Who become the key agents that proliferate the physical, programmatic and spiritual characteristics of the earthen proposal.

The vessel is not only in response to the topical question concerning whether such historical objects should continue to remain in their current circumstances, particularly from a legal and moral standpoint — it also challenges the fundamental conventions of how repatriation can be reimagined. Whilst in opposition to a museum, it operates similarly to an archive, with temple-like characteristics, it conveying the ambience of a divinely spiritual sanctuary. It is a resting place for those passed, sharing some sentiments with a mortuary but rather for figures, that lays atop an animist cemetery, like a typical mausoleum, a monument that encases such within - yet even for the immaterial like a cenotaph.

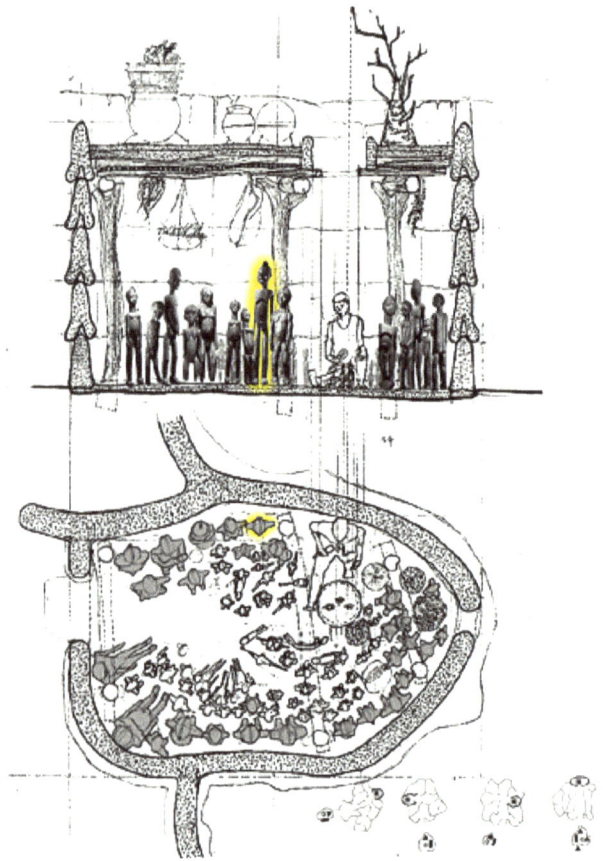

[fig. 1] The earthen dwelling, centred within the Lobi celestial system is grounded and co structed by the landscape.
[fig. 2] The earthen dwelling, centred within the Lobi celestial system is grounded and constructed by the landscape.

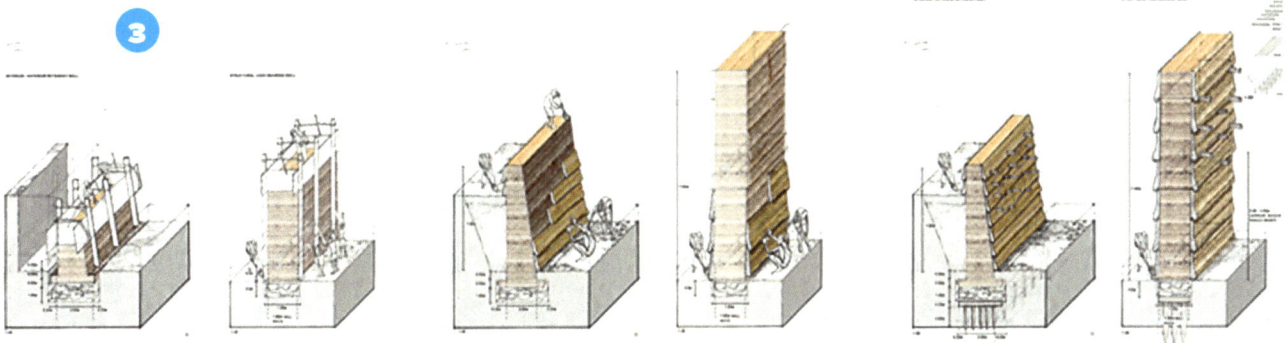

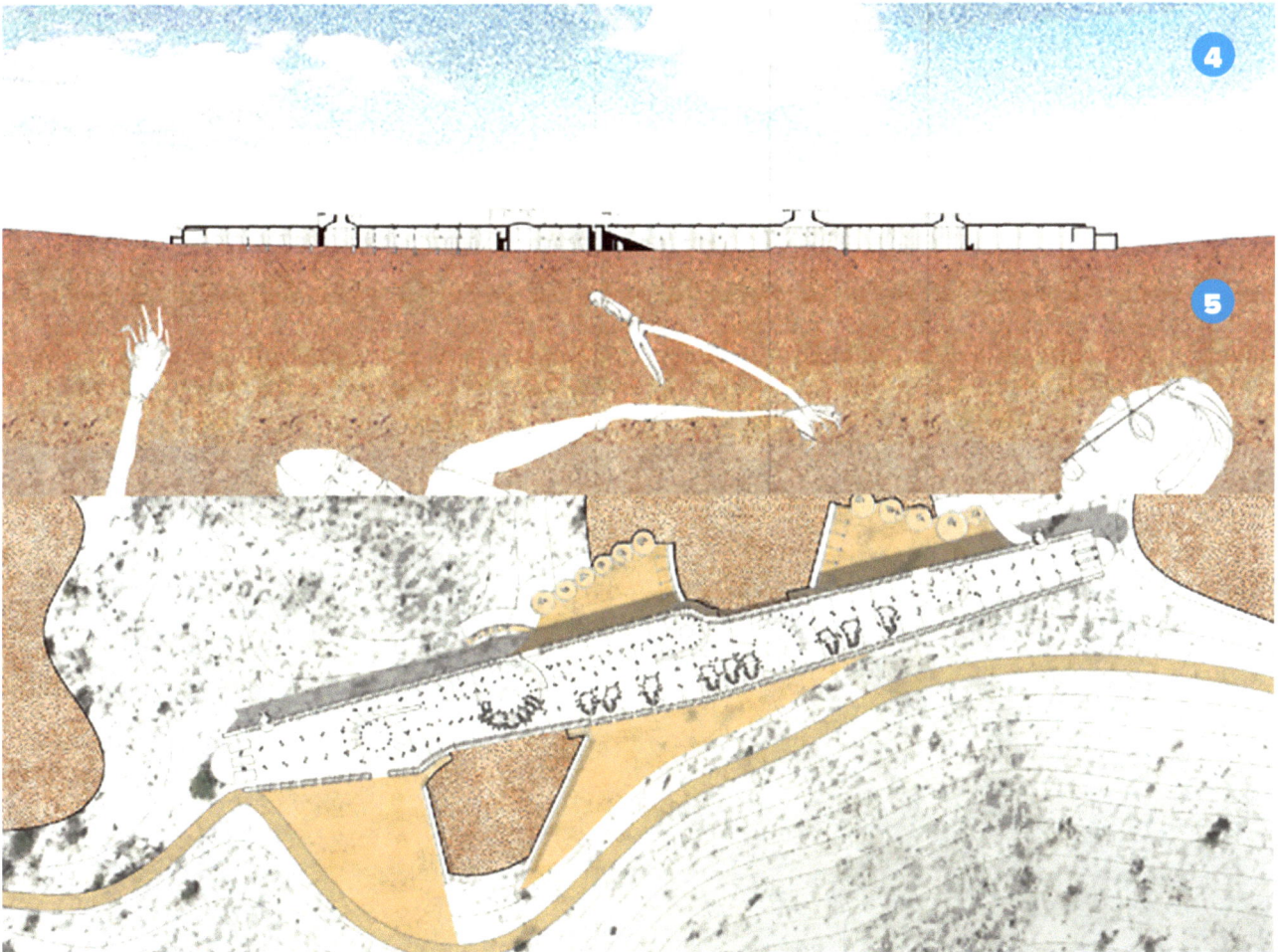

[fig. 3] The walls of the vessel are hybrid combining with the use of a rammed earth core, that is rendered with traditional Lobi banco.

[fig. 4] Long section of the vessel, showing that beneath the landscape - the earth is a final resting place for some repatriated bateba.

[fig. 5] The vessel in plan at ground level, showing the diviner's quarter shrine rooms, seed shrines and outdoor craft enclosures.

[fig. 6] Through the main entrance, the delivery team enter the vessel holding a bundle of repatriated Bateba encased in sealed boxes, turning right, they are led to the circular Diviner's quarter.

[fig. 7] By a light at the end of the proverbial tunnel, meandering between the timber posts, the delivery team leave the moment they place the boxed bateba centrally on the elevated ground

[fig. 8] Only once conclusive information is ascertained through either/both spiritual and metaphysical interpretations; can the Bateba embark on their journey of being reshrined.

[fig. 9] In moments where both physical and divination-based information is deemed inconclusive, the bateba are placed in Flux on long earthen plinths until further notice.

[fig. 10] The excavated enclosed spaces become breeding grounds for bustling creative exchange, promoting the craft of newly invented objects.

[figs. 11, 12 & 13] The earthen vessel embedded within the earthen landscape

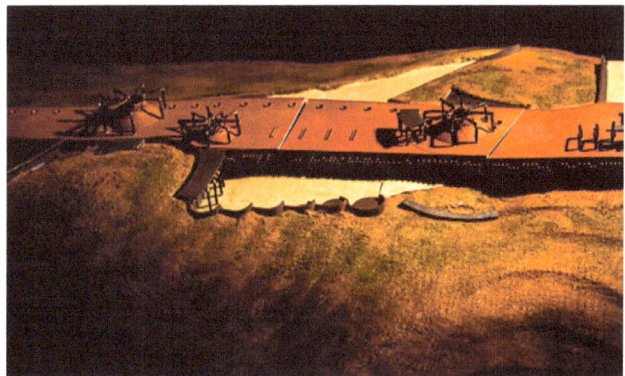

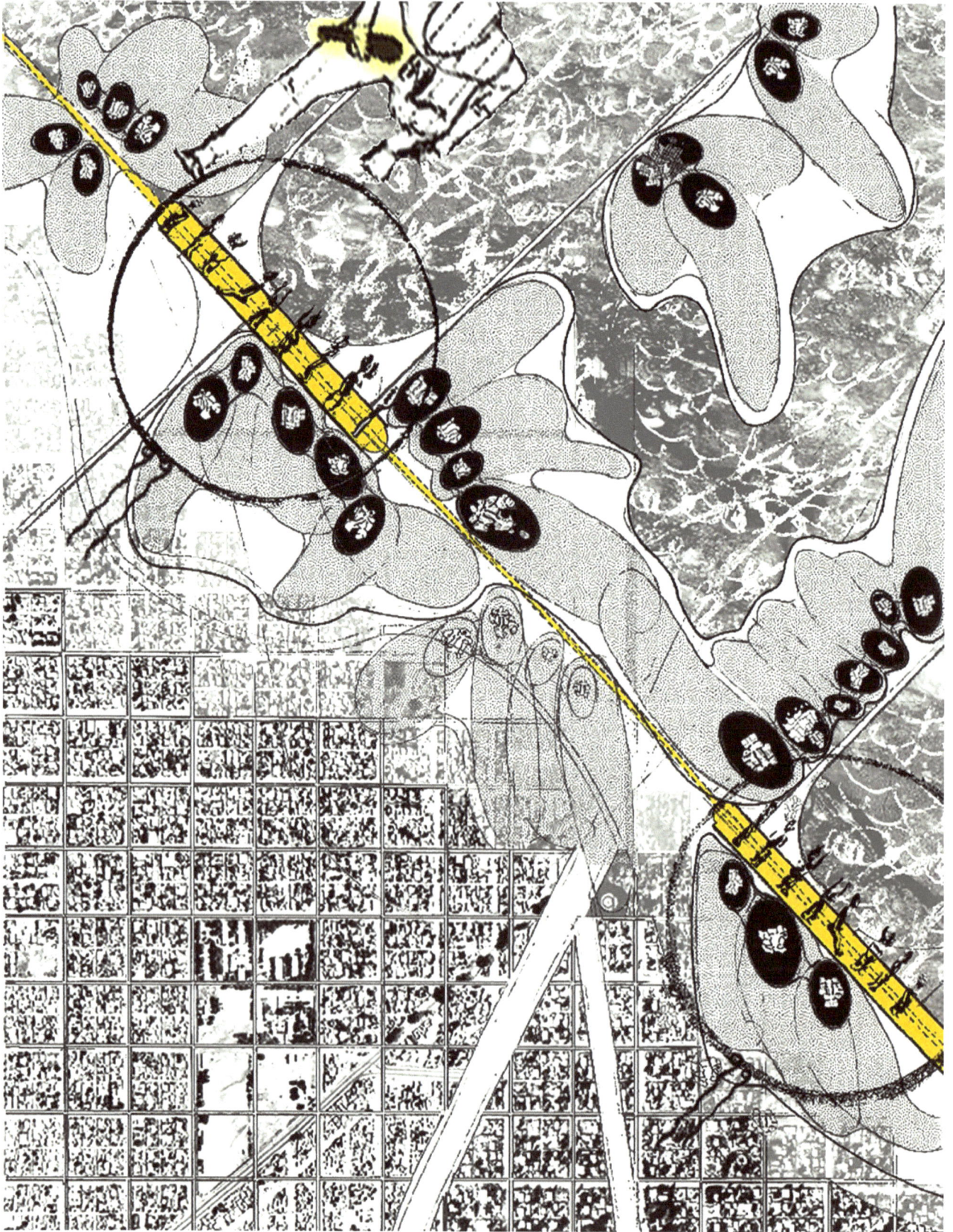

[fig. 14] It is conceivable that well within the next two decades, the expanding boundary pertaining to Gaoua's urban typology will abruptly meet the contemporary vernacular of the Vessel. Speculating, the wider potential of a future West African traditional heritage embedded in urban form.

[fig. 15] Community-based collaborative planning and intervention.

CONCLUSIONS

The Moving African Landscapes project aims to explore the unique meanings of landscapes to individual Africans. Many African cities and communities that were once prosperous and renowned now lie in ruins and memory. Despite this, it's important to revive these cities in our imaginations as they reveal much about the values and habits of the people who made and inhabited them. Unfortunately, African history is often neglected in school curricula and popular media, yet understanding Africa's past is crucial to having a good grasp of world history.

Our first goal is to curate African landscapes from an African perspective, using ethnic languages to connect us to the essence of the space. Our second goal is to become thoughtful analysts of our urban environments, whether historic, cultural, vernacular, or current-day. In this volume, we authors have intuitively expressed their opinions and curated a moving African landscape theme that genuinely reflects the African identity and history. Ultimately, we aim to delve deeper into the attributes of the African landscape and reflect on ourselves as users and travellers within it.

POEM BY
JUSTICIA CAESARIA KICONCO
IS AN ARCHITECT,
FROM UGANDA LIVING IN RWANDA

East Africa's embrace,

a trio of gems, of realms, Kampala, Zanzibar, and Musanze

Each with its charm and story to tell,

A tapestry of cultures where beauty dwells.

Kampala, the heartbeat of Uganda's land,

Where history and culture go hand in hand.

A city bustling with vibrant streets,

Where tradition and modernity swirly meet.

A thriving spirit, a vibrant pace.

Zanzibar, an island of tales untold,

Where ancient history and paradise unfold.

Stone Town's narrow alleys, a maze to explore,

Swahili culture seeping through every door.

Savor the spice markets, taste the ocean breeze,

Zanzibar's enchantment, a treasure to seize.

Musanze, nestled in the Virunga's embrace,

A sanctuary of nature, a serene space.

Where endangered mountain gorillas reside,

A rare encounter, a journey deep inside.

From majestic peaks to twin lakes so serene,

Musanze's beauty, a landscape pristine.

A trio, diverse and grand,

A captivating blend of landscape and nature's hand.

From Kampala's rhythm, to Zanzibar's allure,

And Musanze's serenity, so pure.

Explore the depths of East Africa's charms,

Each destination's allure leaves hearts enchanted.

A scenic backdrop, serene and sublime,

A symphony of nature, frozen in time.

INSPIRATION FROM MY FAMILY

I draw immense inspiration from my supportive family. Justus, Faustah, Jiles, and Judy who consistently encourage my work. Particularly, my grandfather's (the Late Benedicto Mubangizi) profound appreciation for cultural values, his talent as a poet, musician, and exceptional teaching abilities greatly inspire me. Additionally, my parents have beautifully preserved and passed on his enthusiasm for Runyankore and the ankole culture, further deepening my connection to my roots.

ACKNOWLEDGEMENTS

Special thanks to Bernard Atuhaire, Nuwamanya Mariagoretti, Nzahabwanayo Eric, Roger Ntwali, Justus and Faustah Tegyeka, Juditha and Jiles for their invaluable contributions to this poem.

POEM BY
STEPHEN KEKEGHE,
IS A POET AND AN ENGLISH LECTURER, HEAD OF DEPARTMENT AT THE AJAYI CROWTHER UNIVERSITY, NIGERIA

PLUNDERING FEET

They pound their proud feet
on the frail heads of earth's offspring
prowling and poaching little lives--
Greens that seek the sun for survival
now choked and charred
by the plundering feet of poachers

Those who pillage their green neighbors
In restless drives for self and survival
do not know the texture of murder
committed by their crazy feet
on greens of the earth!

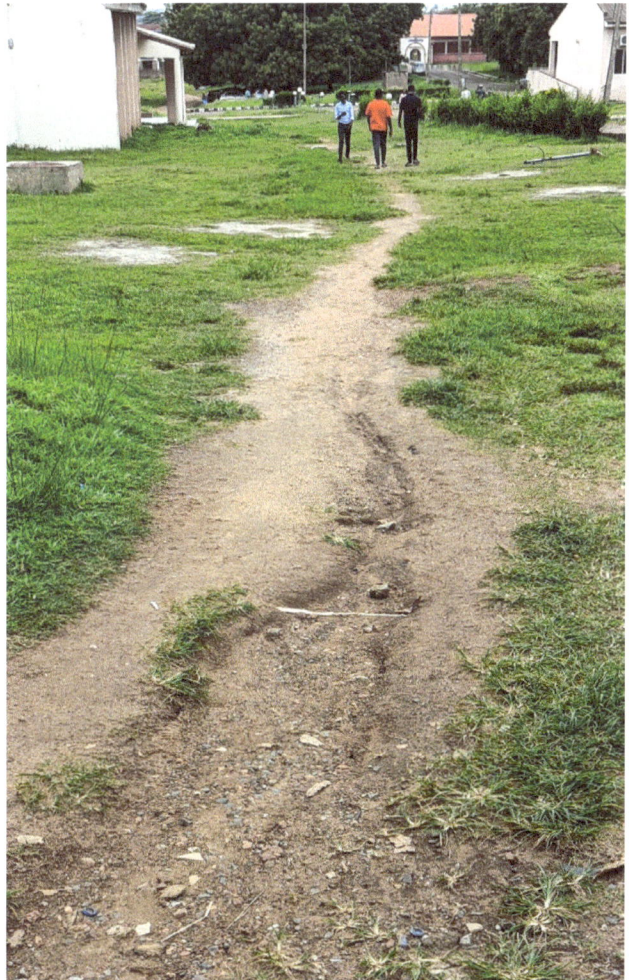

Photos of Ibadan Landscapes by Photographer Daniel Olayiwola based in Ibadan, Nigeria.
University College Hospital, Ibadan Nigeria. Photo Source Daniel Olayiwola, 2022

The Oba Dam, Ibadan Nigeria. Photo Source Daniel Olayiwola, 2022

Aṣẹ!